POEM OF THE YEAR

Clive James

POEM OF THE YEAR

JONATHAN CAPE
THIRTY BEDFORD SQUARE
LONDON

First published 1983
Copyright © 1982, 1983 by Clive James
Jonathan Cape Ltd, 30 Bedford Square, London WC1

British Library Cataloguing in Publication Data
James, Clive
Poem of the year.
I. Title
821   PR9619.3.J27

ISBN 0-224-02961-4

Phototypeset by Wyvern Typesetting Ltd, Bristol
Printed in Great Britain by
Whitstable Litho Ltd, Whitstable Kent

To C. L. Perowne
and the Downhill Badger

Preface

Most narrative verse is written from hindsight. The reader doesn't know what happens next but the writer does. There has always been a place, however, for the kind of narrative verse which turns this relationship back to front, putting the reader in the know and the writer in the dark. In a verse chronicle of unfolding events, the writer can accurately predict very little, whereas the reader will judge from experience. The finest modern example is Louis MacNeice's *Autumn Journal*, a poem one starts off by admiring and then admires more deeply with advancing age. MacNeice could be fairly certain that the autumn of 1938 would bring the Second World War closer, but not of anything else. His personality declared itself along with the events, gaining coherence as they lost it. Rarely has apprehensiveness sounded more human or humanity so worth preserving.

A verse chronicle must be essentially self-revealing. The attitudes struck can easily look ridiculous, and never more so than when struck judiciously, so as to hedge all the bets. The temptation to go back and rewrite is hard to resist. I denied it to myself by publishing my efforts *pari passu* in five separate issues of the *London Review of Books*. The few stanzas which had to be taken out for production reasons I have here put back in. Also I have altered the prosody in several lines which the mother of the dedicatees thought were too much of a challenge to the jaw muscles. One couplet has been rewritten for the good reason that it struck even its author as two matched lengths of haematite. But otherwise the thing is as it was when it was growing in 1982, a year whose events turned out to be beyond anybody's calculations, including those of Nostradamus.

Nobody, certainly not the Foreign Office, knew that Britain would fight a war in the South Atlantic. If you believed in the State of Israel's right to exist, but doubted that Mr Begin was the ideal man to help exercise it, never in your worst memories of Deir Yassin would you have thought that he might let Christians murder Muslims while Israeli soldiers stood by. It was perhaps a fair bet that Mr Brezhnev would grunt his last, but the same bet had been fair for some time. And that Princess Grace would die too was outside the computations of any astrologer.

The only thing the narrator could be reasonably sure of, as the year began, was that the cause of the free Polish trade union Solidarity would be lost before it ended. But there was no telling quite how until it began happening, and then the telling of it was hard on the nerves. *Ottava rima* is not necessarily always a comic form, but it tends that way, and many a time, as the Zomos patrolled in Warsaw or the innocent died bloodily even in the streets of London, I wished I had chosen a stanza inherently more sonorous. But to keep it light was the original idea. Living from day to day, with the television screen bringing us the whole world's grief, we joke to stay sane. If we dwelt on every tragedy it would sound like ours as well as the victim's, and that would be presumptuous. The time to write the elegy is later on, looking back.

Looking back over my longer excursions in verse, I have good cause to thank the editors of those newspapers, magazines and literary periodicals who over the years have given up whole pages to them and sometimes whole issues. Some of these editors thought that what I was doing couldn't be called poetry but they ran it anyway. Their faith

[8]

was an inspiration and the recipient would like to salute them all now, at the moment when he has convinced himself that he is at last, after so much practice, capable of setting down roughly what he means. Ian Hamilton, Claire Tomalin, Anthony Thwaite, Harold Evans, Donald Trelford and Robert Silvers have all, at one time or another, printed extensive concoctions which they knew would earn them letters from serious poets saying that there was a barbarian within the gates. Finally Karl Miller, when faced with the prospect of an entire year in verse, said yes instead of no. It was an instance, negligible on a world scale but looming large for his contributor, of how the individual can affect history. I would never have written this journal without his encouragement. Nor, it might be said, would John De Lorean have ever made that cocaine deal if someone hadn't told him it was a sure thing.

Unpredictability was what made the idea irresistible. It was also what threatened my dedicatees. They watched me scribbling and crossing out until the thing was finished, but in the end they accomplished something just as chancy. They had grown a year older, in a world where no man can be sure that his children will survive the night. In this age which is supposed to be modern, terror hasn't gone away, it has just spread out. Fear now is like gravity: weak but all-pervasive. Reading back over what I have written, I think I can hear it everywhere, and don't know whether to congratulate myself or feel ashamed. But perhaps there are no ways left to take it easy, and all we can do is take it.

London, 1983   C. J.

I

The old year ends with Cambridge under snow.
The world in winter like the Moon in spring
Unyieldingly gives off a grey-blue glow.
An icy laminate caps everything.
Christmas looks Merry if you wish it so.
One strives to hark the Herald Angels sing,
But at each brief hiatus in the feast
A bitter wind howls sadly from the east.

In Poland now the only Santa Claus
Is General Jaruzelski looking grim.
With Solidarity a brave lost cause
There is no father figure except him.
His overall demeanour gives one pause.
Nor are peace prospects really made less dim
By Ronald Reagan recommending firm
Measures that make his Nato allies squirm.

Snow falls again. The atmosphere turns white.
The airfields of East Anglia are socked in.
The atom bombers will not fly tonight.
Tonight the Third World War will not begin.
There's so much concentrated heat and light
Stored around here that if they pulled the pin
The British Isles would be volatilised.
Even the dons would be a bit surprised.

One theory says the Polish Army acted
Only to stop the Russians doing worse.
So clumsily to have a tooth extracted
By family friends calls forth a garbled curse,
But left too long the fang will get impacted
And you won't like the dentist or his nurse.
At least – the pun's not just weak but emetic –
Get the job done with *local* anaesthetic.

Such reasoning is comfortable like us
But soon there are dark rumours to belie it.
The fact the coup has led to far more fuss
Than they say, you can tell when they deny it.
Here in the West we have much to discuss
Beyond the danger to a healthy diet.
You like the thin mints? Try the orange sticks.
Has anybody seen the walnut picks?

Most of the Poles have not got much to eat.
Their democratic leaders have still less.
A cold and cruel and long-drawn-out defeat
Must be the price they pay for small success.
They bucked a system that they could not beat
Which reasserts itself through their distress.
White flakes may decorate the searchlight beams –
The barbed wire is exactly what it seems.

Those men and women braver than the brave
Penned in the open air are telling you
It's better to risk death than be a slave –
Something you thought that you already knew.
And yet to stick together till the grave –
Could we do that if that's what it came to?
One's rather glad one's not cast as a hero
Out there tonight at twenty below zero.

The turkey carcass and Brazil-nut shells
And mandarin rinds fill the pedal bin.
The ice-rimmed church and college chapel bells
Stiffly combine to call the New Year in.
The snow melts and in London the Thames swells
As once the lake lapped Tantalus's chin,
But as I leave the usual filthy train
I guess that the embankments took the strain,

Or else my book-lined eyrie near St Paul's
Would look down on a city rather like
Venice or Amsterdam plus waterfalls
Cascading over many a broken dike.
There'd be ducks nesting in the choir stalls
Of Clement Dane's, and people would catch pike
(With suitably refined outbursts of joy)
From windows at the back of the Savoy.

But there is nothing underfoot save slush
Compounded from crushed ice, old snow and dirt.
Your wellies slurp and gurgle in the mush.
Spat by a taxi wheel the stuff can spurt
Up from the street in one exultant gush
To inundate you where you stand inert.
The cars and buses churn the rhubarb slurry
Until it darkens into cold beef curry.

Schmidt goes to Washington and tells the Yanks
That while his Germany might still be Jerry
The Russians are not Tom and have large tanks
Whose side-effects it can take weeks to bury.
Therefore he is reluctant to give thanks
For Reagan's speeches, which to him seem very
Naive, as if designed to aggravate
The blind intransigence they castigate.

[13]

Congress is humbled by Schmidt's eloquence
Which makes the President sound like an actor
Who reads a script well but is slightly dense
If not as crass as Carter on his tractor.
The Chancellor's impact has been immense.
Intelligence emerges as a factor
In statesmanship and might well start a fashion
Of saying things with point and not just passion.

But whether he is right is hard to judge.
Meanwhile the snow which only last week went
Comes back as if it bore a lasting grudge
And whites the country out from Wales to Kent.
On the M4 the lorries do not budge.
The usual helicopters have been sent
To find the troops last seen the day before
Searching for lost bird-watchers on Broadmoor.

In no time the whole country's ten feet deep:
Landscapes by Breughel, cityscapes by Lowry.
They're using sonar gear to find the sheep.
All Europeans get this as a dowry
But after twenty years I still could weep,
Feeling more foreign to it than a Maori.
I'm half delighted and I'm half disdainful –
It looks so lovely and it feels so painful.

Roy Jenkins will be standing at Hillhead
In Glasgow. The world wonders: is this wise?
Lose Warrington and it's a watershed:
Defeat there was a victory in disguise.
But this time if he doesn't win he's dead
With all his party sharing his demise.
The SDP, awed by its own audacity,
Strikes postures of unflappable sagacity.

[14]

But more of that – much more, no doubt – anon.
Meanwhile Mark Thatcher's managed to get lost
Somewhere in Africa. The hunt is on.
Airborne armadas at tremendous cost
Search all directions where he might have gone.
One tends to find one's fingers slightly crossed.
The days go by and soon it's not a joke.
He's even talked of as a nice young bloke.

Since he in fact is something of a prat
This sudden fondness constitutes a proof
The British heart still beats though lagged with fat.
His mother weeps who once was so aloof
But few there are who take delight in that.
Many who think her son a cocksure goof
And wish her and her politics in hell
Nevertheless in this case wish her well.

The boy is found and instantly reverts
To his accustomed status, that of jerk.
The next blow to the nation really hurts.
ASLEF the footplate union will stop work.
The papers tell us we'll all lose our shirts
Because train-drivers can't forgo a perk.
The sum of Fleet Street's pitiless analysis
Presages chaos, followed by paralysis.

If Fleet Street takes so unified a view
We can be sure the truth must lie elsewhere.
The first train strike of 1982
Inspires more irritation than despair.
Unmotivated locos are not new.
What's fearsome is when planes fall from the air.
In Washington one does. Down on the bed
Of the ice-locked Potomac sit the dead.

[15]

The whole world tuning in through television
For once sees human nature at its best.
A man who might have lived makes the decision
To stay and try to save some of the rest.
Were this a movie, think of the derision
With which we'd greet such an absurd *beau geste*.
On that small screen the big hole in the ice
Frames the reality of sacrifice.

II

The feeling that there's grandeur in mankind
Is soon dispelled by fresh cause for lament.
A rapist is not jailed but merely fined
Because, it seems, the girl was Negligent.
Perhaps the judge has gone out of his mind,
Unless it's him that's straight and us that's bent.
He's set the price for screwing a hitch-hiker:
Two grand. Just toss her out if you don't like her.

Fleet Street, which always disapproves of rape
Despite provoking hot lust on page three,
This time gets on its high horse and goes ape.
In Scotland several men have been set free
Because the woman is in such bad shape
She can't be called on to give testimony.
The man in charge says it's an awkward case.
He's got a point, but no one likes his face.

So Nicky Fairbairn now gets pulled apart
Both in the House and by the public prints.
I must confess I'm not touched to the heart.
That 'style' of his has always made me wince.
I've never liked his haircut for a start,
Nor the sharp trews in which he's wont to mince.
His *Who's Who* entry puts the lid on it:
He has the hide to call himself a Wit.

That title's one which nobody can claim.
You have to wait for others to bestow it.
Not even Oscar Wilde assumed the name,
Who called himself both genius and poet.
That he was self-appointed to his fame –
A true wit wouldn't hint it, much less crow it.
Poor knackered Nicky thinks he's Alan Coren:
He's just a wee laird with a twitching sporran.

And yet it's wise to give conceit expression –
Within the limits set by the absurd.
A boast might be self-serving like Confession
But similarly festers if unheard.
Much meekness stands revealed as self-obsession
When self finds a release too long deferred.
Beware the kind of people who don't flower
Until their shrivelled roots taste fame and power.

Take Henry Kissinger as an example.
The man personifies megalomania.
He's back in action with another sample
Of foreign policy from Ruritania.
On Poland Reagan's harsh words have been ample
But Henry hankers after something zanier.
Leave it to me, he seems to be implying,
And Russian fur will pretty soon be flying.

Suslov checks out. Unless he died of fright
At Henry's rhetoric, it's just old age
That now removes Stalin's last acolyte
And faithful killer gently from the stage.
The mental stature of potato blight
Left him unchallenged as the Party sage:
The perfect man to make sure Ideology
Maintained its power to torture by tautology.

They bury Suslov in the Kremlin wall:
A tribute to his cranial rigidity.
Propped up like that the bricks will never fall.
Meanwhile the intellectual aridity
He helped create still casts its stifling pall:
A dry red dust of cynical stupidity
Ensures the last trace of imagination
Is wept away in hot tears of frustration.

Frustration, but the trains do run on time –
Mainly because the drivers must keep driving
Since any form of strike would be a crime.
No doubt there are time-honoured forms of skiving.
Perhaps their trains, like ours, are sprayed with grime
Before they leave and once more on arriving.
They do, however, go. Without delay.
And what is more they do so every day.

Ours at the moment run five days a week
Or four days, subject to negotiation.
It might be three days even as I speak:
I've lost track of the inverse escalation.
The union leaders talk their usual Greek.
The matter must not go to arbitration.
The strike must bite. The strike days must be staggered.
Sir Peter Parker still smiles but looks haggard.

Sir Peter Parker picked a pickled peck
Of pepper when he took on British Rail.
With every kind of triumph at his beck
And call, perhaps he felt the need to fail.
His chance of saving something from the wreck
Equals his chance to find the Holy Grail.
You never know, though. He and Sidney Weighell
Might possibly cook up some sort of deighell.

If Buckton's ASLEF joined Weighell's NUR
Then BR's board plus ACAS minus VAT . . .
We might as well give up and go by car
Or coach, or on foot if it comes to that.
Some say the train lines should be paved with tar,
Which no doubt counts as talking through your hat,
But if it's true what's needed most is cash
Then stand aside and watch out for the crash.

It's no time to owe money at the bank,
A fact now underlined by Freddie Laker –
Although in part he has the banks to thank
His airline's laid out for the undertaker.
It seems they lent him dough as if they drank
Their lunch directly from the cocktail shaker,
But now the plugs are pulled and in mid-flight
His planes turn back as he gives up the fight.

Disconsolate the DC10s come home
To Gatwick where in time someone will buy them.
An airliner is not a garden gnome.
They can't just sit there. Somebody will fly them.
Defeated legions coming home to Rome
Would choose new emperors and deify them,
But Freddie, though his hearty laugh rings hollow,
Is not an act just anyone can follow.

Sir Freddie, Thatcher's knight with shining wings,
Her favourite Private Sector buccaneer,
Seems to have made rather a mess of things.
Is this collapse the end of his career?
His air of loosely buckled swash still clings.
The cut-price flying public holds him dear.
They send pound notes to keep Skytrain in motion –
Straws in the wind although drops in the ocean.

Here's proof the people value enterprise
And overlook, in those they think have got it,
A Rolls like Freddie's of excessive size,
A house so big an astronaut could spot it.
Whatever shibboleth might galvanise
The public, public ownership is not it.
Despite the very real risk of fatalities
People identify with personalities.

Just when Sir Freddie masticates the dust
The civil servants get their indexed pensions.
Not only Thatcher fans express disgust
At this exposé of the inner tensions
Between what she would like to do and must.
It is an awkward fact she seldom mentions:
The spread she said she'd end of public spending
Increases, and the increase is unending.

She can't trim bureaucratic overmanning.
She cuts the social services instead.
You needn't be as wise as Pitt or Canning
To see how malnutrition lies ahead.
Conversely, Labour's universal planning
Is just the cure to leave the patient dead.
The Alliance must win if it has the nerve to.
At this rate if they don't they don't deserve to.

III

A thought to bear in mind as we now watch
The Labour Party tear at its own guts.
The Peace of Bishop's Stortford's a hotch-potch
Which to place faith in you must first be nuts.
With moulting mane Foot still attempts to scotch
All doubts by well-placed ha-has and tut-tuts,
But while he waffles wanly about Unity
The toughs build up their beachhead with impunity.

The Peace of Bishop's Stortford lulls the press
Which now says it's the SDP that's split.
The lead of the Alliance has grown less,
The tabloids chortle, champing at the bit.
Alliance policies are in a mess
And all in all this new lot aren't quite it.
On Tebbit's union bill they show dissension –
Clear indication of internal tension.

De Lorean the glamour-puss tycoon
Whose gull-wing car is built with our tax money
Might lay at least a gull-sized egg quite soon.
He's suave and clever and his wife's a honey.
For Northern Ireland he has been a boon.
But still and all there's something slightly funny . . .
Or maybe I just find the car too dull,
Attractive only to another gull.

At any rate, the books are with Jim Prior,
Who must decide if we should drop De Lorean
And cut the loss or raise the ante higher.
De Lorean's first name should have been Dorian:
That ageless face of the *Playboy* high-flyer
Is decomposing like an ancient saurian.
I think he's guilty mainly of wild dreams
And now he sees them cracking at the seams.

Prior pronounces. Not another penny
Of public funds. De Lorean must raise
The cash himself. Has he himself got any?
His blink-rate slows to a stunned mackerel glaze.
No doubt he has some rich friends but how many?
He has to find the moola in two days.
Meanwhile the bootlace leeches of Fleet Street
Come sucking up in search of easy meat.

De Lorean finds every well is dry
And Prior duly puts in the Receiver,
Who luckily is not just the one guy
Since lately he's been working like a beaver.
Times Newspapers might be the next to die,
Tossing and turning with the self-same fever.
A mighty panic's on to kill things off.
They're giving the last rites at the first cough.

To think the SDP is on the wane –
While Labour's somehow on the comeback trail –
Unless I am a Dutchman is insane.
I don't say the Alliance cannot fail.
I just say that they cannot fail to gain
If Labour puts itself beyond the pale
By dosing its venereal infection
With Valium until the next election.

[23]

The bubble's burst already. It's revealed
The Militants have plans by which the fate
Of all non-Marxist MPs would be sealed
And power would go leftward on a plate.
All bets are off and it's a battlefield.
Poor Foot is in a terrifying state,
While Benn's grin says with fathomless hypocrisy
That's what you get for holding down Democracy.

The Tendency's great plot, is it a fact?
It could be fake like the Zinoviev letter.
There's something phoney about this whole act.
When people plot red plots don't they plot better?
They can't be nincompoops as *well* as cracked.
You'd get a better plot from a red setter.
They should have signed it with the mark of Zorro.
Perhaps *The Times* will tell us all, tomorrow.

I go to buy my paper the next day
Feeling that every *Times* may be my last,
And meet Neil Kinnock making a *tournée*
Of St Paul's Yard. He's gleefully aghast
At the Red Plot. 'You'd think the CIA
Had written it!' But it was moved and passed
And signed, sealed and delivered through the post
By these dumb-clucks. They've served themselves on
    toast.

Brave Kinnock thinks his cause will by this blunder
Be further armoured in defence of sanity.
I'd hate to see good men like him go under:
So much charm rarely has so little vanity.
But why else is his party torn asunder
If not because the measure of humanity
He represents is deemed not just outdated
But doomed to be hacked down and extirpated?

[24]

For Benn's and Scargill's Labour I won't vote.
For Kinnock's I would think it churlish not to.
Foot knows most voters are like me and float
And that to win them he has simply got to
Keep down the ranters who get people's goat.
He must do something but does not know what to.
Frank Hooley booted out at Sheffield Heeley
And now Fred Mulley too! It's too much, really.

Foot's shuffling feet should be in carpet slippers
But clearly Kinnock remains loyal still.
As he and his nice wife and their two nippers
Pursue their half-term hike down Ludgate Hill,
Threading between the tourists and day-trippers,
They seem to incarnate the People's Will.
I only wish that such a thing existed
And like a cherished building could be listed.

As Amersham achieves Privatisation
And sells the way hot cakes do when dirt cheap
We realise with a sickening sensation,
As of a skier on a slope too steep,
That if the soundest firms owned by the nation
Are flogged, the duds are all we'll get to keep –
And when the auction ends they'll sell the hammer.
We're heading downhill faster than Franz Klammer.

On that one deal the public's out of pocket
Some umpteen million quid or thereabouts.
Thatcher gives everyone concerned a rocket
But *re* her policy betrays no doubts.
Around her neck she wears a heart-shaped locket
In which lie curled some undernourished sprouts
Of Milton Friedman's hair plucked from his head
Or elsewhere during hectic nights in bed.

I speak in metaphor, needless to say:
Milton and Maggie you could not call lovers
Save in the strictly intellectual way
By which they sleep beneath the same warm covers
And wake up side by side to face the day
Throbbing in concert like a pair of plovers –
Though Milty while he shaves sometimes talks tough
And tells her she's not being rough *enough*.

Monetarism as an orthodoxy
Is lethal preached by one like the PM,
Precisely *because* she's got so much moxie.
She burns deep like the hard flame from a gem,
Sticks to her guns like glutinous epoxy,
And views the dole queues others would condemn
As growing proof that cutting out dead wood
Can in the long run only lead to good.

No need to say those millions on the dole
Are there because the Government decrees it.
The contrary idea is a live coal,
A notion so dire that the mind can't seize it.
Suppose that unemployment on the whole
Would be the same no matter what . . . Stop! Cheese it!
Better believe that Maggie acts from malice,
Childishly spiteful like JR in *Dallas*.

An aircraft hijacked in Dar es Salaam
Arrives at Stansted full of Tanzanians.
The Immigration officers keep calm
Almost as if these folk were Europeans.
One wouldn't want to see them come to harm.
Stansted's a long way north of New Orleans.
But dash it all, eh what! What a kerfuffle
Just to sort out some minor tribal scuffle!

[26]

It seems these hijack chappies hate Nyerere
And think that Stansted's the best place to say it.
The SAS are on tap looking scary,
A mighty strong card if we have to play it.
As hijacks go, though, this one's airy-fairy.
The price they ask is vague and kind words pay it.
Believing that their cause is understood
They throw down weapons mostly carved from wood.

A mess on our own doorstep's thus averted.
What started it we fail to comprehend.
Once more we in the plush West have asserted
Our will that awkwardness must have an end.
And yet it's possible that we've just flirted
With some great hurt no words of ours can mend,
In which we might well once have had a hand –
A homing chicken coming in to land.

IV

Speaking of which, one fears that Mr Thorpe
Will not reign long as Amnesty's new chief.
Placed under stress he has been known to warp,
As David Astor points out with some grief.
I must say that Thorpe's nerve gives cause to gawp.
A decent silence should not be so brief.
One does feel he might wear more sober togs
And do things quietly in aid of dogs.

Marcus Aurelius said there's an age
Beyond which we should scorn the public eye,
Put down our seals of office, quit the stage,
Settle our business and prepare to die.
No one denies the emperor was a sage:
His precepts, though, we nowadays defy.
Old Brezhnev, for example, will stay there
As long as there's enough dye for his hair.

Perhaps he's dead already and controlled
Remotely by a powerful transmitter.
Another waxwork poured in the same mould
Might stir up protest or at least a titter.
His chassis, valves and circuits have grown old.
The struggle to replace them could be bitter.
At checking-out time for the ape-faced gremlin
Try to avoid the front desk of the Kremlin.

But just as I write this the rumour's rife
That Brezhnev's had it and the fight is on
For who'll be next to taste immortal life
As General Secretary when he's gone.
Silent arrests and kindred signs of strife
Compose the usual deaf-mute telethon.
One man scores points for standing near another
But drops out when denounced by his own mother.

How droll these thugs would be if not so sad,
Watching their backs and also the main chance.
Most aren't insane or even mildly mad.
Each owns a blue suit with two pairs of pants.
By now they think Marxism was a fad
But still they hold that men should live like ants
While they themselves adorn the doll museum
Standing on top of Lenin's mausoleum.

Blue-jawed top dogs of the *Nomenklatura*
They loom while squads of workers toting spanners
Come stomping by like Nazis past the Führer
Except the signs are different on the banners.
The *idée fixe* is still that a bravura
Performance turns this comedy of manners
Into some species of impressive drama
Instead of just a childish diorama.

According to the *Sunday Times*, Pat Wall,
Prospective Labour MP (Militant),
Has risen on hirsute hind legs to bawl
A vintage load of Jacobinist cant,
Insisting that the Monarch, Lords and all
Such privileged figures strangely yet extant,
Must forthwith holus-bolus be abolished
Or strictly speaking physically demolished.

[29]

Wild Wall includes the judges in his fury,
Which indicates that when he comes to power
As well as MP he'll be judge and jury –
A prospect at which even saints might cower.
The Party handles him as Madame Curie
Handled her radium hour after hour,
Unmindful that the steady radiation
In her own blood and bones worked devastation.

But now South Africa becomes the focus
Of every cricket lover's expert gaze,
While those who think the great game hocus-pocus,
A ritual rain-dance that goes on for days
Until the grey clouds open up and soak us,
This time can only look on in amaze
As British cricketers receive abuse
For being not just tiresome but obtuse.

Boycott, we hear, should live up to his name,
And not be one by whom sanctions are busted.
He and his mates of almost equal fame
Could well prove to have been falsely entrusted
With their credentials in the holy game.
Students of sport pronounce themselves disgusted
Since segregated cricket, in a sense,
Is like denying blacks the sacraments.

Apartheid has not much to recommend it.
What else can it engender except hate?
One day the blacks will find a way to end it
Their masters will not spot until too late.
Meanwhile the sole good reason to defend it
Somebody should be brave enough to state:
With all of the appropriate delights
Top-level cricket is reserved for whites.

[30]

You must be white to wear the proper cap
And have a drink while you watch Boycott bat
And during lunch go down and meet the chap
And slap him on the back and have a chat
And go back up and take a little nap
And finally he's run out and that's that.
Yes, that was Boycott's finest innings yet:
Those fifteen runs that took three days to get.

Boycott was born to give the Wisden bores
The perfect subject for their lucubrations.
He is the average oaf whose average scores
Are averaged out in their long computations,
Reducing you to helpless yawns and snores.
Like small boys spotting trains in railway stations,
They fall into the deep trance of the mystic
Merely by contemplating some statistic.

The Thunderer survives. To celebrate
It seems the editor must walk the plank.
You'd think that Gray's Inn Road was Watergate.
If driving there you should go in a tank.
The building's angled walls of armour plate
Look harder to bust open than a bank,
But in the corridors strong men now stagger
Their shoulders having grown the sudden dagger.

By having Rupert Murdoch as proprietor
Printing House Square hoped for some meed of peace,
But even if at first the storms grew quieter
From disputation there was no release.
And now your average *Times* man thinks a rioter
Is lucky to be fighting just the police,
Such is the measure of the relaxation
Achieved under the Murdoch dispensation.

[31]

When I dispraise my great compatriot
It's not just out of envy for his loot,
Though if it's good he should have such a lot
Still tends to strike me as a point that's moot.
For how his influence sends things to pot,
However, one's concern must be acute.
The centre cannot hold, things fall apart
And everybody ends up in the cart.

Howe's budget pacifies the Tory Wets,
And at the same time seems fine to the Drys.
In other words, the PM's hedged her bets
If only for the breathing space it buys
While everyone who's got a job forgets
Roy Jenkins once was roughly twice as wise
A Chancellor as is Sir Geoffrey Howe –
A fact she'd rather like suppressed just now.

The peace of Bishop's Stortford and Howe's Budget –
In each case the effect might not be meant,
But if it's by the outcome that you judge it
You must ascribe it to the one intent:
Don't rock the party boat or even nudge it,
Bail as a team until the squall is spent,
And when the central threat has blown away
We'll fight among ourselves another day.

At Hillhead Jenkins slips back in the polls.
The press rehearses Doom for the Alliance.
Great play is made with the electoral rolls.
Psephology is cried up as a science.
E'en as the cookie crumbles the bell tolls.
The gaff is blown and fate brooks no defiance.
One question, though, if anybody cares:
How often do *you* answer questionnaires?

Never, of course, because you are too bright,
As most Hillheaders are cracked up to be.
Which could just mean, if I am guessing right,
There's still a vote there for the SDP,
Though if it will be all right on the night
We'll simply have to wait ten days and see,
While Jenkins stands increasingly alone
On those cold concave doorsteps of grey stone.

V

Supposedly a media creation,
The SDP's now patronised in print
From all sides as a hollow aberration,
A candy zero like a Polo Mint.
At best such lofty talk's an irritation,
At worst it sets the heart as hard as flint,
But summed up it must prove, if Jenkins conquers,
That stuff about the media was bonkers.

Columbia flames spaceward from the Cape,
Aboard it a glass box of moths and bees.
As Jenkins makes a last lunge for the tape
The press and pollsters are in agonies.
The free-fall moths still buzz in tip-top shape.
The bees just hang there looking hard to please.
Both moths and bees go nowhere in a hurry,
Bees in a sulk and moths in a fine flurry.

So what's the point of effort in that case?
Why didn't old Roy stay home and write books
Instead of pounding through this paper chase,
The sweat of which does little for his looks?
The bees have got the right approach to space:
The moths flap uselessly like fish on hooks . . .
The tension's fearful and one feels no better for
Committing such a thoroughly mixed metaphor.

[34]

The die is cast but does not yet lie still
And while it rolls it's hard to count the dots.
The shape of politics for good or ill
Lies in the gift of a few thousand Scots
Of whom a certain element will fill
Their ballot papers in with jokes and blots –
But that's Democracy and worth preserving
Although at times incredibly unnerving.

Roy Jenkins wins and history is made
Or if not made at least it's modified.
The dingbats straight away are on parade
With Benn at his most foam-flecked and pop-eyed,
Saying the SDP has overplayed
Its hand and now must go out with the tide.
Thus King Canute spake as his feet got wetter,
But further up the beach his court knew better.

But now a comic opera interlude
Wins our attention from domestic cares.
The generals in the Argentine, though rude
And cruel and prone to giving themselves airs,
Have in the foreign field so far been shrewd,
Confining lunacy to home affairs.
Their latest coup arouses less admonishment
Than universal open-mouthed astonishment.

The Falkland Islands taken by invasion?
So what's there to invade excepting sheep?
It's no great wonder that on this occasion
The Foreign Office got caught half asleep.
Deuced awkward that the natives are Caucasian
And what is more, we're told, resolved to keep,
Though so far flung in crude terms of locality,
All ties intact of British nationality.

[35]

Storms in a teacup are a sign of spring
And few can take the Falkland business seriously.
Wavers of flags will have their little fling,
Diehard imperialists will speak imperiously,
And one sincerely trusts that the whole thing
Will fade away the way it came, mysteriously.
Meanwhile by long tradition Oxford's won
The boat race and there's been whole hours of sun.

Dick Saunders at the age of forty-eight
Wins the Grand National. Excellent result.
We raddled crocks excitedly spectate
Dismissing youth as no more than a cult.
The horses nose-dive at a frightful rate.
It's carnage yet one can't help but exult
As David Coleman, fiftyish and cocky,
Congratulates 'the oldest winning jockey'.

Nobody wants to be a fading power
And countries are like men in that regard.
A nation brushed aside as past its hour
Even if that is true will take it hard.
The sceptic courts a sojourn in the Tower
Of London with a yeoman as a guard.
War fever mounts. All one can do is watch it
And hope that this time our side doesn't botch it.

The Secretary of Defence, John Nott,
Has made a whopping balls-up in the House.
The Foreign Secretary's on the spot,
Loudly accused of being short of nous.
The top gun-boat exponent of the lot,
A prancing lion where once crouched a mouse,
Is Michael Foot, who now speaks for the nation
In this alleged Hour of Humiliation.

[36]

Lord Carrington presents the dazed PM
With his own head upon a point of honour.
The nitwit Nott stays at his post pro tem
Though in the long term he must be a goner.
Poor Thatcher makes a mighty show of phlegm
At all the bad luck that's been heaped upon her,
Announcing, as the Fleet prepares to sail,
We must not even *think* that we might fail.

Such rhetoric is brave if weirdly phrased,
Though fustian it's backed up by legality,
Yet what can't help but leave you slightly fazed
Is the persistent air of unreality.
Those china eyes of hers were always glazed
But now have the glaucoma of fatality,
As if what happened on the field of Mars
Could somehow be predicted by the stars.

Proud ancient Athens sent a sure-fire mission
So strong it could not fail to overawe.
Its name was the Sicilian Expedition.
It lost them the Peloponnesian War.
Ill fortune and long distance worked attrition
Not even the most timorous foresaw.
Thucydides was there and for posterity
Wrote down the consequences of temerity.

As those Greeks at Piraeus in the dawn
Cheered when the galleys raced towards Aegina,
Our patriots now lean on the car horn.
The little motor-boats from the marina
Are teeming in each other's wash like spawn.
All wish the Fleet fair winds for Argentina.
Invincible looks worthy of its name.
The battleship *Repulse* once looked the same.

[37]

I don't doubt our atomic submarines
Can sink their diesel ones in nothing flat.
We sold them all our second-best machines
And man to man should put them on the mat.
But time and place are with the Argentines:
Say what you like there is no blinking that.
We'll take two weeks to get to where we're going —
Which means that until then there's just no knowing.

Two weeks of spring in England, with the hedges
Acquiring flowering hawthorn like dried snow.
The lawns with rows of daffodils at the edges
In Cambridge look too succulent to mow.
I'm told at night they jack them up on wedges
And pull the grass down slightly from below.
Millions of tourists sip at a serenity
Made all the sweeter by the world's obscenity.

Two weeks in the museum and the garden
That some say bitterly Britain's become.
They say Dutch elm disease is rife in Arden.
Britannia's teeth have grown loose in the gum.
The brain gets softer as the arteries harden.
There's too much store set by detached aplomb . . .
So think the vitalists and spoil for action,
Finding in hesitation no attraction.

Two weeks go by and there's no other news
Except what centres on the vexed Malvinas.
If UN Resolution 502's
To mean a thing the next move's Argentina's.
The Yanks, alas, are either short of clues
Or scared of being taken to the cleaners.
Al Haig, while six quacks monitor his ticker,
Sits on the fence through which his allies bicker.

South Georgia falls to us with no life lost.
Our Fleet is justly proud but Fleet Street's prouder.
The jingo hacks want war at any cost:
Abaft cleared desks they perch on kegs of powder.
At last the US gets its wires uncrossed.
Sighs of relief are heaved but somewhat louder
The first bombs fall. It may or may not suit you,
But those who are about to die salute you.

VI

As fifty thousand people in Warsaw
March for Walesa and for Solidarity,
They rate, beside the South Atlantic war,
The same space as a fun run staged for charity.
The Falklands dwarf even El Salvador,
Which ought to be a ludicrous disparity,
But clear-cut issues fought out to a finish
Have sex appeal no slaughter can diminish.

Port Stanley's airstrip is the first thing hurt,
Bombed by a Vulcan and a pack of Harriers.
No skin and hair fly with the grass and dirt.
Unharmed back to Ascension and the carriers
Go all the planes. This war seems snugly girt,
Like some Grand Prix, with crash-proof safety barriers.
It would be fun to watch it on TV
Instead of that chap from the MOD.

You couldn't call the way he talks laconic,
Which mainly means not to be too effusive.
What few words come from this guy are subsonic.
While waiting for the point you grow abusive.
And yet it adds up to a national tonic
For reasons which to my mind prove elusive,
Unless based on a firm belief that God
Speaks to one people and spares them the rod.

[40]

Indeed the other side is first to find
Even a sand-tray war costs full-sized lives.
Summoned by noise of a familiar kind
The Exterminating Angel now arrives.
Perhaps, although like Justice he is blind,
It riles him that the gauchos fight with knives:
At any rate, they are the ones he picks
To prove that punctured ships go down like bricks.

Their cruiser the *Belgrano* takes a hit
Opening up her side to the cold sea,
Which enters in and there's an end of it.
Hundreds of sailors either can't swim free
Or can but freeze, and prayers don't help a bit,
Nor raise the temperature by one degree.
The fire is just to burn those who don't drown
As too full of young voices she goes down.

This is the finest hour of *Mail* and *Star*.
The *Sun* especially is cock-a-hoop,
Shouting commands as if at Trafalgar.
Swab out the trunnion cleats and caulk that poop!
What terrifying warriors they are,
These slewed slop-slingers of the slipshod sloop
El Vino, which each lunchtime takes them south
Into the raging gales of the loud mouth.

A scrivener myself, I should not gripe.
The natural consequence of a free press
Must be that hacks are well paid to write tripe.
One normally feels more scorn than distress
At clichés ready set in slugs of type,
But this exceeds the usual heartlessness:
Faced with a raucous clamour so mind-bending
You wonder if free speech is worth defending.

The war dance falters. Foam dries on the lips
As word by drawn-out word the news comes through:
The *Sheffield*, one of our most modern ships,
A spanking, Sea Dart-armed type 42
Destroyer built to wipe out radar blips,
A Space Invaders expert's dream come true,
Is hit. With what's so far an untold cost
In lives. Has burned. Is given up for lost.

An Etendard released an Exocet
Which duly skimmed the waves as advertised.
Our tabloids wring what mileage they can get
Out of French perfidy, but undisguised
Is their amazement such a classy jet
Flown by these dagoes that they've patronised
Should leave the runway, let alone deliver
This thing so clever that it makes you shiver.

Imagination, if it slept before,
Is now awake and fully occupied
By what's occurred and still might be in store.
With closed eyes you can see the way they died:
The bulkheads hot as a reactor core,
The air the same to breathe as cyanide.
And now that the grim news has got us thinking,
Think of the *Canberra* broken-backed and sinking.

With all at risk there is a pause for thought,
But lest the nation's troubled heart grow faint
El Vino without ever leaving port
Fires paper salvoes that confer the taint
Of Traitor on the doubtful. All those caught
Equivocating must dodge yellow paint
Which flies in dollops like wet chamois leathers
Whilst air-burst cardboard shells disgorge white feathers.

[42]

My own view is we ought to go ahead
Even though press support brings only shame.
But my view's that of one with a warm bed
While others face the shrapnel and the flame.
What can you do except note with due dread
The other side in this case are to blame
And would, unless constrained to go away,
Keep what they took though talking till Doomsday?

Such elementary thoughts make me feel dull.
Rarely is it so simple to be right.
But for the nonce there is a blessed lull.
It's possible the UN still just might
Ensure we've seen the last cracked-open hull
And fighter plane turned to a fire in flight.
The mind, robbed of its surfeit of raw action,
Spoiled for the real now searches for distraction.

Snooker on television is the moral
Equivalent of war. Man against man,
It is a pitiless yet bloodless quarrel
Racking the nerves behind the deadened pan.
Slowly a break accumulates like coral
Yet has the logic of a battle plan.
Fought out on a flat sea within four walls
Well has this conflict been called chess with balls.

This year the final's between two ex-champs.
Veteran Ray Reardon's cool, calm and collected,
While Alex Higgins twitches and gets cramps
Whenever from his headlong rush deflected.
I'd like to keep a foot in both these camps,
Believing the two styles, deep down, connected.
They fight it to a finish frame by frame
And no one doubts it's more than just a game.

[43]

Higgins has won and as the fuss subsides
We realise that a game is all it is:
A fish-tank show of strength by fortune's tides,
A show-case for old smoothness and young fizz,
Where Reardon's neatly brushed short back and sides
Bow out with good grace to a lank-haired whizz,
And from the Crucible, their battlefield,
Nobody needs to go home on a shield.

But now on Friday, 21st of May
We hear what happens in a proper fight.
Eight thousand miles south in San Carlos Bay
The invasion has been going on all night.
Men on both sides have really died today.
The bridgehead's been wide open since first light.
Out in the Sound our gun-line ships pump flak
Through which their planes fly low to the attack.

I'm speaking as an armchair strategist
Who's been through every scrap since Marathon
When I suggest (some colleagues would insist)
Amphibious assaults are just not on
Unless you've got the air clasped in your fist.
This is the biggest gamble since Inchon,
And there the Yanks had more planes than they knew
Quite what to do with. We've got precious few.

Not that the Harrier falls short of being
A modern miracle of engineering.
When it performs you can't grasp what you're seeing:
A frisbee fork-lift truck with power steering,
It floats, flies backwards, stem-turns as if skiing –
The thing's a runabout for Wilma Deering.
The Argentines are suitably outclassed
But still get through by going low and fast.

No pictures except those in the mind's eye
Exist to give some inkling of the scene.
The Skyhawks and Mirages come mast-high,
We're told, but must suppose what those words mean.
Our rockets rush to burst them as they fly
Like thrown milk bottles full of kerosene,
But back along their line of flight the bay
Seeded by bombs grows tall white trees of spray.

So it goes on but can't go on forever
Without ships hit by something worse than spume.
Brave pilots die in swarms but their endeavour
Is part-rewarded when a bomb finds room
Inside the frigate *Ardent*, there to sever
Her spinal column like a lowered boom.
We're also told they've hit the *Antelope*
But that bomb was a dud and she can cope.

VII

It wasn't. Twenty hours from being struck
The *Antelope* erupts in the dark night.
Having no pictures might be our good luck:
Without doubt it's a mesmerising sight.
The mere sound is enough to make you duck,
But what might really make us choke with fright
Would be to see the troopships the next morning
Still looming there in spite of that grim warning.

Ashore in strength, our soldiers now advance.
The Pope's at Gatwick with the same intention.
It could be said he's taking the same chance
Of getting shot, but let's not even mention
That possibility as the slow dance
Of ritual opens with his condescension
To kiss the tarmac, which this osculation
No doubt excites to transubstantiation.

The Popemobile moves off on its campaign
Of conquest, firing fusillades of prayer.
Appropriate response I find a strain,
Suspecting that this pontiff talks hot air
And only got the part when Michael Caine
Turned cold on the long frocks he'd have to wear.
But thousands of young Catholics seem delighted
As if he were the Beatles reunited.

Without fail every rock-concert-sized crowd
Goes mad while the old boy lays down the law.
It seems that birth control's still not allowed.
Also he deeply disapproves of war.
His fans are all too busy being wowed
To search these propositions for a flaw.
He might as well be singing 'Love me tender'.
They shout and put their hands up in surrender.

Soon now the Argentines will do that too.
Their Skyhawks still punch large holes in our fleet
But in Port Stanley they must know they're through.
The paras and marines slog through the peat
Towards them looking too tough to be true.
A chilling enough spectre of defeat
To make those poor young hungry conscripts wary
About the last stand promised by Galtieri.

Reminding us that it's not over yet
The *Coventry* is lost and in Bluff Cove
The prospect that has always made one sweat
Comes true. The Skyhawks find their treasure trove:
A loaded troopship, which they promptly set
Ablaze like a defective petrol stove.
We're given just the name, *Sir Galahad*.
No figures, which suggests they might be bad.

That was the nightmare from the very start,
The sea full of drowned soldiers, but the dread
Is dulled by distance to a thing apart.
Israel's ambassador is left for dead
In London, which one tends to take to heart.
He lies there with a bullet in the head.
Israel strikes north into the Lebanon
And instantly another war is on.

Reagan rides into London looking grey
Around the gills at how the world is going.
By this, of course, I do not mean to say
His make-up's worn off and the real skin's showing:
Just that the outer pancake's flaked away
To show the thick foundation wanly glowing,
Cracked by his smile of disbelief at meeting
Lord Hailsham dressed for the official greeting.

If Reagan's jet-black hair seems slightly strange,
What about Hailsham's wig, sword, socks and cape?
The President when dressed to ride the range
Looks odd, but not as weird as a square grape.
For Reagan it must make at least a change
Wondering how they let this nut escape,
As backwards Hailsham goes with a low bow
Showing him where the boys sit down to chow.

The Falklands war ends and Galtieri falls:
His hawk-like features drawn as a wet sheet,
He takes a minimum of curtain calls
And finds, outside the stage door in the street,
That though his mouth continues to spout balls
His tears have made mud pies of his clay feet,
And so he has to crawl instead of walk
Home to a house full of his empty talk.

One counts the hundreds dead in the Atlantic
And feels regretful at the very least,
But as wars go it rated as romantic
Beside the shambles in the Middle East,
Where thousands are dead, maimed or driven frantic
As round Beirut the steel squeeze is increased.
Some say the Jews have been transmogrified
To Nazis, and that this is Genocide.

One doesn't have to be a Zionist
To spot the weakness in this parallel.
Begin strikes me as still the terrorist
He started off as and a fool as well,
But bad though things now look, one must insist
That war is war. The Holocaust was Hell.
For Begin, children's deaths seem incidental.
For Adolf Hitler they were fundamental.

The Nazis sought complete obliteration,
Women and children being top priority.
The PLO's a warlike armed formation
Whose goal – we have it on their own authority –
Is Israel's disappearance as a nation.
No nonsense about rights for the minority,
Just dumb insistence that the hated state
Should make its mind up to evaporate.

The Jews won't sit still twice for being slaughtered.
The Palestinians will fight to live.
Justice and mercy will be drawn and quartered.
Things will be done a saint could not forgive.
The towns and cities will be bombed and mortared
Until like hot sand they fall through a sieve,
And on the day that blood turns into wine
There will be peace again in Palestine.

My biblical locutions you'll excuse:
The Royal Birth, if not a new Nativity,
Is everywhere regarded as Good News
Except by those of levelling proclivity
Who think the common folk do not enthuse
At such shows of élitist exclusivity
From choice, but somehow cheer because they've got to,
Being by glamour too bedazzled not to.

[49]

War-leader Thatcher, having proved her nerve,
Now rants of a new spirit sweeping Britain,
But peace is not war and high talk won't serve
For long to stop the biter getting bitten.
Let's hope the lorries don't run short of derv:
Even as this last couplet's being written
The London Tube strike's trumped by British Rail,
Which stops dead too but on a larger scale.

A Borgless Wimbledon soaks up the rain
Which falls like a monsoon arriving late.
Al Haig resigns with every sign of strain:
Someone called Shultz is now in charge at State.
The new prince is named William. The odd train
Starts up again as if to celebrate,
But ASLEF thinks a moving train just fosters
Flexible notions with regard to rosters.

Ray Buckton therefore plans a whole new strike.
Meanwhile the members of the SDP
Mark ballot slips to name the man they'd like
To lead them on the stroll to destiny.
The polls and press say Roy will need a bike:
Young Owen's gone too far ahead to see.
Fuelled by the Falklands Factor Owen's flowered
And left Roy looking rather underpowered.

Most members of the SDP, however,
Joined in the first place to see Roy PM.
No question Dr Owen's very clever:
The elder statesman's still the man for them.
They vote to prove the Falklands business never
Made hazy the true *terminus ad quem*.
The thing that matters is the next election,
Not smart young David's feelings of rejection.

[50]

Though disappointed, Owen takes it well.
One might just say the same for McEnroe.
Outplayed by Connors he does not raise hell
But mainly hangs his head in silent woe.
He lurks like a sick crab in a dull shell.
His only tantrum is to drag his toe,
And when a cross-court drive goes nowhere near it
Say 'fuck it' where the umpire cannot hear it.

Jimbo I've always thought was mighty good.
It's nice to see a champion come back.
But McEnroe, we're told, is such a hood
That when he can't run haywire he goes slack.
He should have smashed his racket to matchwood
And used the jagged handle to attack
The umpire, linesmen, ballboys, Duke of Kent
And so on till his bottled wrath was spent.

For McEnroe, Release of Pent-up Tension
(I quote Mark Cox, player turned commentator)
Is fundamental to the whole dimension
Of polished touch akin to Walter Pater
Which makes John's game so marvellous the mere
    mention
Of his resemblance to an alligator
Can only mean that genius is beyond us –
Unless, of course, the little bastard's conned us.

VIII

Off home flies McEnroe in deep dejection,
His face a sweet potato cooked in steam.
But this time his behaviour bore inspection,
The usual nightmare merely a bad dream.
One looks upon him almost with affection
And hopes the British World Cup football team
Will similarly take the setback stoically
If it transpires they don't do so heroically.

A goalless draw with Spain wipes out the chance
Britain was in with. Miffed at how we muffed it,
The British fans, deprived now of romance,
Regain the sad hotels in which they've roughed it
And ponder at great length the fact that France
Was the one team to whom we really stuffed it.
Many a fan's bald head shows the deep crease
Made by the impact of the Spanish police.

Young men of Britain sleep now at Goose Green
In plastic bags lined up in a long grave.
Large speeches were engendered by that scene
Of how our Comprehensive lads were brave.
But now, as if the war had never been,
The thrill is gone and when yobs misbehave
In youthful ways that tend towards the strenuous,
Thatcher's New Spirit looks a trifle tenuous.

A young man penetrates Buck House by night
And duns the Monarch for a cigarette.
It's her behalf on which we all take fright,
Loath to admit the idea makes us sweat
Of some dark whisper asking for a light . . .
But this chill prospect's easily offset,
For though the endless train strike makes you chafe
It means rail travel's absolutely safe.

The man who shook the Queen down for a fag
Is nabbed and named unsmilingly as Fagan.
Though young, it seems he rates as an old lag.
He's got a dossier on him like Lord Kagan.
He's dropped in several times to chew the rag
And strolled around at leisure like Carl Sagan.
An expert on the Palace architecture
Perhaps he wanted her to hear him lecture.

The police, alas, were clueless by comparison.
One of the cops was in bed with a maid.
While as for all that military garrison,
It turns out they do nothing but parade.
You'd think that they might detail the odd Saracen
To park outside her bedroom . . . Feeling frayed,
The Queen perhaps is not best placed to hear
Her personal detective is a queer.

No doubt she sort of sussed but did not mind,
Certain at least the poor klutz wasn't chasing
The tweenies, but now that the clot's resigned
So publicly, it must be less than bracing
For her to know the best men they could find
To guard against the danger that she's facing
From acid, knife, gun, gas, napalm and bomb
Had rings run round them by a peeping Tom.

Foot plumps for ASLEF but as if in spite
The TUC does not and the strike's broken.
Foot's coiffe should go a purer shade of white
Unless his fiery gesture was a token
To make him look a tough nut in a fight
For all those gritty doctrines he has spoken
On that day when they have to be renounced
And Arthur Scargill's strike bid must be trounced.

But Arthur's rhetoric is like his hair.
Though spurious, transparent and bombastic,
It's legal and has some right to be there.
The threat it poses to the state is drastic
But one democracy's equipped to bear.
He's less fanatical than he's fantastic.
That puff-ball pan's so openly ambitious
Only a stocking mask could make it vicious.

Indeed his nimbus of elated strands
Bespeaks not just the patience of a saint
But holiness. It balances no hands.
The halo Giotto botched with thick gold paint
On Arthur's a UFO that never lands,
A cap of gossamer you might find quaint
But can't deny has something brave about it —
He's sparing us the way he'd look without it.

The real and lasting threat to national sanity
Has no objection to remaining nameless.
Among its vices you could not count vanity.
On that score its participants are blameless.
They aim to wake your sense of shared humanity
By perpetrating outrages so shameless
That you will grant a view must have validity
Which gives rise to such murderous stupidity.

In Knightsbridge a car bomb with up-to-date
Remote controls proves powerful competition
For horsemen wearing plumes and silver plate,
While up in Regent's Park a similar mission
Is carried out with a success as great,
Ensuring, at the moment of ignition,
Musicians who have never hurt a soul
Are shown up in their true repressive role.

For what's a bandsman, when all's said and done,
If not a soldier of a certain sort?
What is a trombone but a type of gun?
What is a bandstand but a kind of fort?
Objectively, the difference is none:
These men were troops no matter what they thought,
And as for sleepy listening civilians —
They symbolise the acquiescent millions

Who now unquestionably come awake
And wonder for a week stretched to nine days
If this is not more than the nerves can take.
The horses' wounds bared to the public gaze
Cause many a grave thoughtful head to shake.
Dumb pain is real but how strange that it weighs
Thus heavily, when humans ask what mattered
So much it left them or their loved ones shattered.

Did Cromwell's ruthlessness bring this to pass,
A woman crawling with a face of blood?
Did the Earl of Essex raise a storm of glass
When he set fire to houses of thatched mud?
A bugle boy for being armed with brass
Was pricked to die. What caused that? The Great Flood?
The grievous debt goes back to the beginning
That makes these men more sinned against than sinning.

[55]

The guilty live, the innocent lie dead:
The summer sun shines warmly on them all.
In Biarritz it shines on my bald head.
My scalp accepts the photons as they fall.
No Scargill I, I let my skull turn red,
Building my daughters a thick sand sea wall.
They crouch behind it, clinging to the notion
Somehow their father can control the ocean.

I can't stop waves, or much else, reaching them.
Relieved they're not in Belfast or Beirut
I'm flattered in a way some might condemn
To find their sense of beauty so acute.
Each shell's looked at as if it were a gem,
Held to the ear, then blown on like a flute.
By those too young to know the world is cruel
A cured sea-horse is treasured as a jewel.

The London papers bring the usual news —
Inflation's down yet unemployment climbs.
But here the gulf's laid out in greens and blues:
Lapis, fresh lettuce and the juice of limes.
Lulled by the heat one's body cells refuse
To wait for the return of better times:
They take their holiday though deprivation
Should devastate the luckless British nation.

The spirit's willing but the flesh is weak.
Skin will be free and easy if it can.
Through down-turned mouth with deep concern we
    speak:
The epidermis has its selfish plan
To look less like the thick end of a leek.
The height of its ambition is a tan.
For two weeks while the tide goes up and down
I watch it and react by turning brown.

[56]

In Biarritz the sun sets like a peach
That ripens and ignites towards the water.
Waves which were blue like denims when they bleach
Turn silver as a newly minted quarter.
Absorbed by darkness outwards from the beach,
Like lemon ice licked by my younger daughter
White light is ineluctably consumed,
Ripples erased. Desired and therefore doomed.

Something fulfilled this hour, loved or endured –
A line of Auden's that burns in the mind.
By now just like the sea-horse I am cured.
Having acquired a dark and brittle rind,
I feel resigned again, if not inured,
To how the real world out there is unkind,
As flying back to it I read Camus
Amazed how he continues to come true.

The innocent, he once wrote, in our age
Must justify themselves. That still sounds right.
The Jews in Paris now take centre-stage.
A restaurant is reamed with gelignite.
The elders might express old-fashioned rage
But modern anti-Semites are more polite,
Claiming that Zionism must be fought
Wherever Jews might offer it support.

Thus reason the Jew-baiters of the Left
As once the Right spoke in *Je suis partout*.
The warp's formed by the same thread as the weft:
Woven together, they are what they do.
Between them there's no fundamental cleft,
A fact appreciated by Camus
Whom both sides honoured with their deepest hate –
In my view a most enviable fate.

IX

In Britain the health workers strike for pay
Which surely in all conscience they've got coming.
The harvest's in and farmers stack the hay.
Around the rotting fruit the wasps are humming.
The CBI says Thatcher must give way.
It's all so soothing, not to say benumbing.
England is now and history is elsewhere.
Most of the rough stuff isn't here, it's there.

It's there in Israel where General Sharon
Even by Begin's found intransigent.
In Gdansk the water cannon are turned on
As if cold spit could wash away cement.
Now Arafat with all his options gone
Concedes perhaps it's time his people went.
The PLO might recognise Israel.
The Poles pretend Walesa's not in gaol.

But history here at home is the two Krays
Let out of clink to mourn their saintly mother.
The boys for all their rough-and-tumble ways
Both loved her as they never loved another.
People repaired with grafts, pins, splints and stays
Still can't decide which was the nicer brother –
The Kray who'd chat you up before he grabbed you
And held you helpless, or the Kray who stabbed you.

[58]

The other big event is Poet Sue,
A scribbling Cambridge undergraduette,
Who as the French once went mad for Minou
Is cried up as the greatest talent yet
By dons who should have better things to do,
You might think, than to stand there getting wet
Drooling about the girl's supreme facility
For sonnets of Shakespearean fertility.

It seems she churns them out like a machine
That manufactures plastic souvenirs,
And on the whole that's roughly what they mean:
They're so banal you can't believe your ears.
They echo everything that's ever been
Created in the last five hundred years.
Sue's poor brain is a boneyard, a Sargasso,
A pulping mill, a collage by Picasso.

The dons who praise her were once Leavisites,
Slow to admire and vicious in dismissal.
What aberration has brought on these flights
Of rapture as they cluster round a thistle
And call the thing a rose and spend their nights
Composing articles that make you whistle,
Since even Leavis's worst panegyrics
For Ronald Bottrall didn't sound like lyrics?

The dons are punished for their dereliction
With dour gibes from the joyless Donald Davie
Who demonstrates at length Sue's vaunted diction
Tastes thin compared with dehydrated gravy,
While as for her alleged powers of depiction . . .
The dons must feel they've been shelled by the Navy.
He calls them symptoms of a deep malaise
As Cambridge English falls on evil days.

[59]

But dons were ever shaky in their taste.
Davie himself is nuts for Ezra Pound.
It's not on judgment their careers are based.
They tend the fields but they break no new ground.
Old Leavis thought that writers could be 'placed'
Even while they still lived and moved around.
Alas, he was so tone-deaf that his scrutiny
Made spinning poets in their graves plot mutiny.

The reason why the dons find Sue prodigious
Is patent when you see a photograph.
No wonder they forgot to be prestigious:
The girl's so pretty that she makes you laugh.
I trust no don involved will get litigious
For being likened to a love-sick calf –
I understand completely how the urge'll
Emerge to call a virgin a new Virgil.

A summer madness that began in spring
The Sue Affair's explained by a don's life.
His winter schedule is a humdrum thing
And often the same goes for the don's wife.
Though every day the sweet girl students bring
Their essays which he goes through like a knife,
The whole deal's on the intellectual level
And busy hands do no work for the Devil.

But then the crocus drive up to the sun
And Sue puts on a floating cotton dress
And that fine friendship as of priest and nun
Erupts into a secular distress.
Those sonnets that she turns out by the ton
Must mean the girl's a gifted poetess:
Sue's such a doll she'd make Professor Carey
Say that she wrote like Dante Alighieri.

Sue's bubble reputation having popped
Her teachers must wipe soap out of their eyes,
But one would hate to see those young wings cropped
Merely because her mentors were not wise.
If that compulsive gush of hers is stopped
It ought to be because she's learned to prize
The disciplines that temper and anneal,
Growing slow blooms of strength inside the steel.

There's energy in Sue's headlong slapdash
Which most of our young careful craftsmen lack.
They watch their language and do nothing rash.
Crushed in the boot and wound tight on the rack,
Pressed thin with weights and strung up for the lash,
Each poem is a puzzle that must crack,
Yielding its meaning drop by anguished drop
Until, drained dry, it dies with a full stop.

One image per two stanzas is the ration,
Though some there are who don't risk even that.
Such level surfaces are hard to fashion.
It takes a kind of built-in thermostat
To ward off sudden puffs of wayward passion
Which might cause pimples in what should be flat,
Protected in all possible directions
Against the threat of critical objections.

Better to write in quite another style
And be accused of sentimental clowning.
Better to court the condescending smile
Of that drear ghost still droning on in Downing.
In Italy for all too short a while
I grapple with the greatest work of Browning.
What chance would it have stood against those wits
Of our day whose chief skill is to pick nits?

[61]

But even Browning sweated for more density
Than line could hold which brain could still retain.
Astonished by the man's sustained intensity
I see the packed force of that hardwood grain,
But find his tapestry's compressed immensity
Undone by a pervading sense of strain:
The book runs such tight rings around itself
No wonder it sits heavy on the shelf.

Perhaps there's now no hope of being clear
Unless one's also hopelessly naive;
An air of easiness is bought too dear
If cheap effects are all it can achieve;
But in Ferrara I stand very near
The kind of art in which I can believe –
That generous tribute to a mean employer,
Cossa's great frescoes in the Schifanoia.

Faded to pastel they're still full of light.
Each panel has an effortless proportion.
It's love of life that makes those faces bright.
The skill is consummate without distortion.
Sure of its knowledge like a bird in flight,
Such perfect freedom feels no need of caution,
And so the teeming polychrome quotidian
Enjoys perpetually its just meridian.

But just only as art. Injustice then,
As rank as now, had no redress at all.
Below those stately dames and lolling men
A Jew sprints for his life across the wall,
Insistently reminding you of when,
In recent days still well within recall,
So many innocent were naked runners
Towards the mass graves and the machine-gunners.

X

The past gives solace and rededication
But offers no escape from harsh reality.
Back in the present, all one's information
Suggests the air of gracious informality
The Quattrocento brought to relaxation
Would now seem strained whatever the locality –
There are no independent city-states
Equipped to keep the world outside their gates.

From West Beirut into the waiting ships
The PLO pulls out on television.
With gestures of one cashing in his chips
According to some tactical decision
Their leader puckers those unlovely lips,
But only fools would whistle in derision
As his sad captains all get kissed goodbye –
Mere military defeat won't stop *that* guy.

I must say he's no oil-painting, Yasser,
Or if he is then it's of something weird.
Nothing would make him look as good as Nasser
But still you'd think he'd try a *proper* beard.
For head-gear an entire antimacassar
Arranged so that his features disappeared
Would do more than that tea-towel does at present
To make his aspect generally more pleasant.

One day no doubt he will be played on screen
By some young ringer for Alain Delon.
Most people look at odds with what they mean:
We're bound to simplify them when they're gone.
Golda Meir's reported to have been
Transformed by Ingrid Bergman to a swan,
But now, with Bergman dead at sixty-five,
No one in *Casablanca*'s left alive.

It was a clumsy film with a bum script
Yet watching it once more I sit and dream.
The cigarettes they smoke aren't filter-tipped.
Bogie pours whisky in a steady stream.
Small vices. It's by virtue they are gripped.
Of self-indulgence there is not a gleam.
She wavers but he has the strength of ten
As time goes by and Sam plays it again.

Reagan and Thatcher ought to be like that.
Instead they have a frightful falling-out.
The Russian pipeline has inspired the spat,
Or that's what spokesmen *say* it's all about.
In private Maggie's spitting like a cat.
In public, as per usual, she says nowt,
Calling the USA our greatest friend
While thinking its top man the living end.

Scargill and Benn say let's break Tebbit's law.
Jim Callaghan less bluntly says that too.
Israel and Syria might go to war.
The boggled mind wonders what else is new.
In Berne the Polish Embassy's front door
Is opened while some breakfast is pushed through:
The terrorists are hauled out bearing traces
Of the omelette which has blown up in their faces.

[64]

But wait a second. Don't you find it odd
So dumb a move comes from pro-liberal Poles?
Are these a self-selected awkward squad
Or has the other side smartly switched roles?
To keep Walesa endlessly in quod
It might help if more tender-hearted souls
Thought *Solidarnosc* meant armed insurrection
Against the Party's warm clasp of affection.

It's possible one's getting paranoid:
Walesa's just too big to disappear.
But murder's been a frequently employed
Political technique in this past year.
To show the Government what to avoid
Sicilian *mafiosi* arouse fear
By gunning down the general sent to face them
Before he even gets a chance to chase them.

Dalla Chiesa's death convinces me –
I think that all in all and on the whole
I won't go righting wrongs in Sicily.
Nor will a few lines praising a brave Pole
Do very much to set his people free.
Perhaps a phantom quest's the one sane goal –
As now the *Sun* claims to have found Lord Lucan
In deepest jungle with tapir and toucan.

The Jungle Fugitive's a Fleet Street thriller
That Martin Bormann starred in last time round.
Embezzler on the lam and missing killer
Swathed in lianas are abruptly found.
One day no doubt they'll bump into Glenn Miller,
So many scribes are covering the ground.
He'll be with Harold Holt and all the rest
Back to the crew of the *Marie Celeste*.

No news is good news and fake news is fun
Or would be if the bad news caused less strain.
To stop us laughing too long at the *Sun*
Another DC10 comes down in Spain.
The Lebanon's Gemayel lived by the gun.
He puts the gun down and is promptly slain,
While in her palace chapel Princess Grace
Too soon lies dead in high-necked silk and lace.

Our big affair was over years ago
And merits no more than this brief report.
I claimed her for my own in *Rear Window*
And from the Odeon walked lost in thought
The long way home exuding love's hot glow.
Believing Rainier was far too short,
I gave her up in fury mixed with grief
The seventh time I saw *To Catch a Thief*.

Flying above Beirut towards Bombay
By night en route to faraway Peking
One's well aware that earlier today
Down there the corpses were still quivering.
The most the Israelis are prepared to say
Is that the Christians had their little fling
Unsupervised, with awkward consequences
For Muslims not equipped with barbed-wire fences.

Thousands of blameless people lying dead,
The State of Israel's credit well-nigh wrecked,
And all of it on Begin's bullet head
Who should have seen his duty to protect
Civilian lives if his invasion led
To the point where each and every local sect
Was tempted to vent pent-up animosity
By staging the odd small-scale mass atrocity.

[66]

The least that Begin and Sharon can do
Is step down and donate their brains to science.
What few friends Israel has left urge them to
But neither hero seems moved to compliance.
The Knesset is a Hebrew hullabaloo,
The blunderers are childish in defiance,
But for the nonce I put off shame and pity
Standing entranced in the Forbidden City.

For Mrs Thatcher's visit the Chinese
Have laid on a Grade Three official greeting.
Which doesn't mean the bum's rush or the freeze:
She gets an honour guard at the first meeting.
But not much bunting flutters in the breeze.
Tian'anmen Square contains no special seating.
Instead there is a lot of open space
With here and there a mildly curious face.

She's here to pin them down about Hong Kong.
She'd like to have a written guarantee.
The PM's habit is to come on strong.
The Chinese instinct is to wait and see.
Any idea the business won't take long
Ebbs when the welcome turns out so low key.
China in that respect remains immutable –
The people speak Chinese and look inscrutable.

The Great Hall of the People is the venue
For a fifteen-course State Banquet every night.
There isn't any need to read the menu:
You take a pinch of everything in sight.
It all tastes at least wonderful and when you
Happen upon a dish that's sheer delight
Just go on eating while they bring you more.
They'll keep that up until you hit the floor.

[67]

Shown how by locals in black Beatles suits
We find out what to chew and what to suck.
First having added sauce and onion shoots
We fold the pancake round the Peking Duck.
Maddened by fish lips and sliced lotus roots
The journalists eat like a rugby ruck.
Even our diplomats up there with Her
Tuck in so fast their chopsticks are a blur.

A thousand million ordinary Chinese
Are outside staunchly doing what they're told.
They'd never even dream of meals like these.
It's luxury for them just to grow old.
From dawn to dusk the streets swarm with belled bees.
I hire a bike and join them, feeling bold
And bulking large against the average male
As if I were a wobbly, two-wheeled whale.

Petite they are and easy on the eye,
This quarter of the world's whole population.
The same seems even more true in Shanghai.
Each city stuns you like a whole new nation.
They march together under a red sky
Towards a dream of human transformation.
It's awe-inspiring yet one has to say
One's heart goes out still to the Student Wei.

Young Wei it was who, raised as a Red Guard,
Looked back on his achievements with remorse.
With Mao set to cash in his Party card
Deng and the boys announced a change of course.
The Student Wei invited ten years hard
Saying they'd got the cart before the horse:
If freedom came first, progress might begin.
He pulled his ten years and five more thrown in.

[68]

XI

If only freedom had a sharper taste.
In Hong Kong kneeling by my father's grave
It's not of his life I regret the waste
But my life he kept safe by being brave.
Even in slavery he was not disgraced,
But self-reproach goes through me like a wave
For all the precious daylight I let spill
While he lies tightly locked in that steep hill.

As Thatcher's VC10 with me aboard
Spears up and doubles westward from Kai Tak
At 30,000 feet I still feel floored
By China and make large plans to go back.
It wasn't Communism I adored:
It was the beauty too refined to crack
From history's hammer blows, and yet possessed
In common, everywhere made manifest.

I never knew the sky was full of dust
Above Peking and turned plum at sunset
While all the palace roofs acquired a crust
Of crumbling honeycomb. If I forget
The details or confuse them as one must,
That first sigh of assent is with me yet.
In China though the mind recoils offended
One's visual range can't help but be extended.

With due allowances, the same's applied
To local artists since the Shang at least.
No bronze bell has been cast or silk bolt dyed
If not with reference to the visual feast
Spread out what still must seem the whole world wide
Each day that dawns where else but in the East?
A boundlessness which suffers no real border
Except the outline of an ideal order.

Sung pictures fix my dreams of public art:
Intensely subtle, spaciously compact,
Produced by an élite not set apart,
The theory left implicit in the fact,
A measured naturalness felt from the heart,
The intellect controlled by natural tact —
Schooled to the limit yet prepared to meet
Half-way the average cyclist in the street.

The cyclist, one need hardly add, sees few
Fine paintings from one year's end to the next,
But still the small extent to which his view
Of local architecutre has been vexed
By modern public buildings must be due
To precepts found in no official text,
And least of all in Mao's Little Red Book —
Which you can't buy however hard you look.

Yes, Mao has been reduced from god to man.
He's back to being ordinary flesh.
His mausoleum's small extractor fan
Must now work overtime to keep him fresh.
The Party's cranking out a whole new plan
In which, they say, the word and deed will mesh.
Good luck to them and let's hope Wei gets sprung
In time to share the wealth while he's still young.

[70]

We've flown so far that distances deceive
But back in the real world we left behind
The demonstrators march through Tel Aviv
Sharon and Begin still have not resigned,
But ask their best young people to believe
They never had a massacre in mind.
It must be true since who'd be such a klutz?
Which leaves you thinking they must both be nuts.

There's uproar in the Bundesrepublik
As Schmidt's brought down. Some say he'll get back in
Stronger than ever, others he's so weak
There's just no chance that he can save his skin.
These latter prove correct. Schmidt's up the creek
Without a paddle and Herr Kohl must win.
All those refreshed by Schmidt's astringent attitude
Must now adapt to Kohl's gift for the platitude.

Though Kohl's arrival means there's one bore more
The nett effect seems no worse than narcosis.
We know from sub-Orwellian folklore
That bombast by a process of osmosis
Corrupts the social fabric to the core,
That rhetoric is verbal halitosis —
And yet one still tends to be more afraid
Of forthright men who call a spade a spade.

In Rome some group propounding the belief
That baiting Jews is simply common sense
Creates the optimum amount of grief
By firing shots at minimal expense
Into a crowd of worshippers. Though brief
The sense of satisfaction is intense:
Just one dead child can seem like a whole lot
When that's the only pogrom that you've got.

[71]

You know just where you are with men like these.
They say they want to kill you and they mean it.
In Ireland when they nail you through the knees
You know they've got a point because you've seen it.
Be grateful there are no more mysteries:
Thugs hold the slate and you must help them clean it.
You wanted honest politics? They're here.
Answer the door. What have you got to fear?

In Poland where all terror's state-controlled
The time for Solidarity has come
To be outlawed. Leaders left in the cold
Until their lips turned purple and tongues numb
In dribs and drabs are let loose to grow old
As proof it's wiser to be deaf and dumb
When there's few friends outside to be inspired
And room for them inside if so desired.

But though the days are quicker to grow dark
In Europe now the year starts bowing out,
The flow of dreadful news lifts up an ark
Of hope as all good men combine to shout
Hosannahs for Prince Andrew and Koo Stark,
Who when the chips are down are not in doubt
That what needs doing when the world looks bleak
Is best done on the island of Mustique.

Too bad that jealous Fleet Street crabs the act.
Andrew deserves a break with his show-stopper,
In view of all the dreary weeks he hacked
Around the Falklands with his lonely chopper.
Nevertheless you have to face the fact
Young Koo's the next thing to a teenybopper:
Highly unsuitable and, if adorable
From certain angles, all the more deplorable.

[72]

Page Three pin-ups and skin-flick clips of Koo
Are dug out so the Palace might take note
That Koo viewed in the long term just won't do
Though in the short term she would stun a stoat.
We're told the Queen has carpeted Andrew
And warned him not to act the giddy goat.
How do the papers get this information?
Let's hope not by nocturnal infiltration.

Gdansk erupts but Martial Law's imposed
To boost the standard military rule.
The Lenin Shipyard wound is not quite closed
But treatment nowadays is prompt if cruel.
The Zomos leave the area well hosed
With noxious matter flushed down the cesspool.
When Jaruzelski reads the fever chart
He'll see the outbreak stymied at the start.

At home the NUR's lost Sidney Weighell.
The SDP has lost points in the polls.
For parties needing TV time I feel
It's mad to have a Conference that Rolls
Instead of staying put, while the appeal
Of packing up each night as for the hols
Is hard to see, unless they're taking pains
To prove that Shirley Williams can catch trains.

More serious than polls for the Alliance,
Roy's Statutory Incomes Policy
Is greeted with a vote of non-compliance,
Thus demonstrating that the SDP
Is not just for a gang of famous giants
But ordinary folk like you and me –
Stout thinking, yet the move, if not divisive,
Can't help at this stage seeming indecisive.

[73]

But John De Lorean shows more than strain
In several parts of that uplifted face.
The handcuffs induce shame on top of pain
As in Los Angeles he falls from grace.
Busted with many kilos of cocaine
Packed neatly in a custom pig-skin case,
He's proved his gull-winged dream car always flew
On snowy puffs of powder from Peru.

And there but for the grace of God go I
Who also in an excess of belief
Am swept up in wild schemes that I swear by
And feel the impact when they come to grief.
But then the raucous critical outcry
Condemns one as more mountebank than thief,
Unless one deals with state funds like De Lorean
And fiddles them like Sallust the historian.

The artist when he claims the Right to Fail
Just means the risk he takes is a sure bet.
Success occurs on an eternal scale.
The lack of it we instantly forget.
The man of action's not free to avail
Himself of such a useful safety net:
He bites the sawdust with the floodlights shining.
The crowd stays put to watch the vultures dining.

XII

A fact which Arthur Scargill demonstrates
By calling on his Membership to strike.
Most of the men down mines are Arthur's mates –
He fights on their behalf and that they like,
However much his bumptious manner grates –
But now they tell him to get on his bike.
From lower chin to fairy-floss beret
His visage holds more egg than a soufflé.

You'd almost think 'poor Arthur' were it not
That Solidarity's new riots show
How little chance a free trade union's got
Once fear is planted and has time to grow.
There's no need nowadays to fire a shot.
Just make them run. They've got nowhere to go.
The hoses gush, the truncheons rise and fall
And where a thousand marched, a hundred crawl.

The movement is just two years old today
And looks already paralysed with age.
That fine collective courage drains away
Into a helpless, inward-turning rage.
The price of protest gets too high to pay.
You shake the bars but cannot shift the cage.
Only the young can be brave as they wish
When one-time physicists are selling fish.

Atomic bombs are our first-string defence
Against all this. A reassuring sign
Is that they're backed up by Intelligence:
From GCHQ any foe's phone line
In two ticks can be tapped at his expense.
A man employed there says it works just fine,
And if he sounds a trifle well-rehearsed
It's just because he told the Russians first.

One secret, though, the Russians couldn't keep
A moment longer even if they tried.
Brezhnev might well be more than just asleep.
It's reasonably certain he has died.
The time has come for crocodiles to weep
And stir the bucket of formaldehyde.
The last spark has winked out in that great brain
Which once did Stalin's work in the Ukraine.

Andropov of the KGB emerges
Inevitably as the next big cheese.
In Hungary he supervised the purges
Which taught them just how hard the Bear can squeeze.
But now it seems he has artistic urges
And intellectual proclivities.
At speaking English he is Leslie Howard:
At playing the piano, Noel Coward.

There's consolation in a fairy-tale,
But none when Lech Walesa is released —
Surely the final proof that he must fail.
In back rooms as a species of lay priest
He might say mass but only in a pale
Reflection of that sacrificial feast
When Poland at the hour of dedication
Tasted what life is like in a free nation.

In Congress Reagan loses the MX
Because they don't think much of the Dense Pack —
A grand scheme calculated to perplex
Red rockets as they swoop to the attack.
Them critters will collide and break their necks.
Some will run wild and others will head back
To blow the roof off the Politburo.
Remember John Wayne and the Alamo!

But there will be, should our blue planet burn,
At least some shred of reason for the fire;
There's just no guarantee we'd ever learn,
Try as we might, to live behind barbed wire;
So threat and counter-threat, though they might turn
The stomach, are not terminally dire —
Although we say it sitting in a crater
The aim was to talk first instead of later.

Someone thinks otherwise in Ballykelly.
A pub explodes and falls on those inside.
The whole platoon of soldiers blown to jelly
Must constitute a cause for secret pride.
Those girls who should have been home watching telly
You'd have to say committed suicide,
An act which no true Christian can condone.
So ends the news-flash from the battle zone.

Ken Livingstone has failed to uninvite
The IRA to meet the GLC.
The Fleet Street hacks with ill-concealed delight
Pour hot lead on his inhumanity.
I like his gall but question his eyesight.
When looking at his newts what does he see?
You'd think that his pop eyes could count their eggs.
No doubt he'd spot it if *they* lost their legs.

[77]

In Florida the last month of the year
Is balmier than England was in June.
There's wild hogs in the boondocks around here
And manatees asleep in the lagoon.
Launch Complex 39's the stack of gear
That fired the first Apollo at the Moon.
Beside Pad A the storks pose poised to scuttle
At any sign of life from the Space Shuttle,

Which stands on end all set to hit the trail
Out of this charnel-house that we inhabit.
It's an ejector seat on a world scale.
Given just half a chance who wouldn't grab it?
Sit still for the volcano up your tail
And you'd be off and running like a rabbit –
Till upside down, a baby before birth,
Floating in silence you would see the Earth.

Earth shows no signs of us viewed from up there
Except the Wall of China, so no wonder
It looks a vision in its veils of air,
The white opacities we hear as thunder
Braided with azure into maidenhair –
It's those conditions we are living under.
That stately clockwork of soft wheels and springs
Keeps time whatever mess we make of things.

Back in the London frost I pile up drifts
Of crumpled A4 as I type my piece.
Some halfwit has been spitting in the lifts.
The thieves patrol more often than the police.
I head for Cambridge with the children's gifts,
Walk down a street made loud by sizzling geese
And am appropriately stunned to see
The work continues on our Christmas tree.

[78]

An angel where there used to be a star.
Twin tinsel strings like stage-struck DNA.
The leaves peel off the Advent calendar
Uncovering one chocolate every day.
The decorators may have gone too far
In hanging Santa Claus from his own sleigh.
Behold two members of the privileged class –
The young, who think that time will never pass.

Too soon to tell them, even if I knew,
The secret of believing life is good
When all that happened was the scythe spared you
While better men were cut down where they stood.
My fortunes thrived in 1982.
I'd have it on my conscience if I could,
But next year will be time to make amends
For feeling happy as the old year ends.